PIONEERS IN THE WORLD OF WEATHER AND CLIMATOLOGY

PIONEERS IN THE WORLD OF WEATHER AND CLIMATOLOGY

EDITED BY SHERMAN HOLLAR

Britannica®
Educational Publishing

IN ASSOCIATION WITH

ROSEN
EDUCATIONAL SERVICES

Published in 2013 by Britannica Educational Publishing
(a trademark of Encyclopædia Britannica, Inc.)
in association with Rosen Educational Services, LLC
29 East 21st Street, New York, NY 10010.

Distributed exclusively by Rosen Educational Services.
For a listing of additional Britannica Educational Publishing titles, call toll free (800) 237-9932.

First Edition

Britannica Educational Publishing
J.E. Luebering: Director, Core Reference Group, Encyclopædia Britannica
Adam Augustyn: Assistant Manager, Encyclopædia Britannica

Anthony L. Green: Editor, Compton's by Britannica
Michael Anderson: Senior Editor, Compton's by Britannica
Andrea R. Field: Senior Editor, Compton's by Britannica
Sherman Hollar: Senior Editor, Compton's by Britannica

Marilyn L. Barton: Senior Coordinator, Production Control
Steven Bosco: Director, Editorial Technologies
Lisa S. Braucher: Senior Producer and Data Editor
Yvette Charboneau: Senior Copy Editor
Kathy Nakamura: Manager, Media Acquisition

Rosen Educational Services
Jeanne Nagle: Rosen Editor
Nelson Sá: Art Director
Cindy Reiman: Photography Manager
Karen Huang: Photo Researcher
Brian Garvey: Designer, Cover Design
Introduction by Jeanne Nagle

Library of Congress Cataloging-in-Publication Data

Pioneers in the world of weather and climatology/edited by Sherman Hollar.—1st ed.
    p. cm.—(Inventors and innovators)
"In association with Britannica Edicational Publishing, Rosen Educational Services."
Includes bibliographical references and index.
Audience: 7 to 8.
ISBN 978-1-61530-702-9 (library binding)
1. Meteorologists—Biography—Juvenile literature. 2. Climatologists—Biography—Juvenile
literature. 3. Meteorology—History—Juvenile literature. 4. Climatology—History—Juvenile literature.
I. Hollar, Sherman.
QC858.A2P56 2013
511.6092'2—dc23
                                                                      2012008580

Manufactured in the United States of America

On the cover: A Doppler radar tower stands in relief of an approaching storm. *Dean Kerr/Shutterstock.com*

Interior background image © iStockphoto.com/Tatjana Rittner

CONTENTS

INTRODUCTION

NEW YORK
×
72W
68W
CLOUDS
SHELF
EDDY
HINGTON
SLOPE
EDDY
× NORFOLK
NORTH WALL
GULF STREAM
EDDY
EDDY
SARGASSO
SEA

Infrared image showing temperature variations in the Gulf Stream, taken by a National Oceanic and Atmospheric Administration satellite. Science & Society Picture Library/Getty Images

Anyone who has ever planned an outdoor event, dressed in layers to accommodate seasonal temperature changes, or wondered whether he or she should grab an umbrella on the way out the door knows that the weather can be unpredictable. Throughout history, many scientific minds have risen to the challenge of understanding and explaining the natural phenomena of storms, weather fronts, and climatic changes. It is these pioneering individuals whom this book celebrates.

Early weather-related scientific discoveries often came about as the result of exploration of other matters. The ancient Greek philosopher Aristotle wrote the *Meteorologica*, a famous essay on meteorology, while studying the natural world and pondering the universe. Galileo, who is most famous for his work in astronomy, invented the thermometer while teaching physics at the University of Padua. Neither Daniel Fahrenheit nor Anders Celsius had studying the weather as their main goal, yet each had a temperature scale he had devised named after him.

There also were "renaissance men" such as Benjamin Franklin and Joseph

Henry, who were accomplished in many fields. Meteorology was just one of many areas in which they made a mark. Their contributions to the atmospheric sciences are well-documented, especially Franklin's famous experiment with a kite flown during a thunderstorm to test the electrical properties of lightning.

Yet several of the pioneers featured in this book have dedicated their professional lives specifically to the study of weather and climate. These are the people who have conducted the research and created the tools that have advanced the fields of meteorology and climatology. Among their number is Wladimir Köppen, whose charting of world temperatures led him to divide the world into climate regions—a landmark event in climatology.

It could be said that other weather and climate pioneers had their heads in the clouds, in the best possible sense. Swedish meteorologist Tor Bergeron was known for his work in cloud physics, specifically regarding the question of how precipitation occurs. American Vincent Joseph Schaefer was not merely content to study clouds. Instead, he sought to control their output. In 1946 Schaefer conducted the first successful cloud seeding, which involves treating clouds with chemicals to produce snow or rain.

Humankind's influence on the weather didn't end there. By the middle of the 20th century, scientists were beginning to understand that changes in climate were linked to human activity such as the burning of fossil fuels. In 1958, climatologist Charles David Keeling began measuring carbon dioxide levels near an inactive Hawaiian volcano. His findings showed that CO_2 levels were rising, which scientists claim is one cause of global warming. As chairman of the United Nations Intergovernmental Panel on Climate Change (IPCC), Swedish meteorologist Bert Bolin helped raise awareness of the dangers of climate change. In 2007 the IPCC shared a Nobel Peace Prize with former U.S. vice president Al Gore.

It is unlikely that anyone will ever be able to predict the weather with 100 percent accuracy. But thanks to the efforts of these pioneers and others like them, there are far fewer mysteries in the worlds of meteorology and climatology than there once were.

CHAPTER 1

ARISTOTLE

The ancient Greek philosopher Aristotle, one of the greatest thinkers of all time, wrote the world's first meteorological treatise, *Meteorologica*, in the 4th century BC. *Meteorologica* remained the standard work on the subject for 2,000 years.

Born in 384 BC in Stagira, on the northwest coast of the Aegean Sea, Aristotle was the son of the physician who tended to the king of Macedonia. As such, the boy spent plenty of time at court. At 17, Aristotle enrolled at the famous Academy, directed by the philosopher Plato.

Aristotle threw himself wholeheartedly into Plato's pursuit of truth and goodness. Plato was soon calling him the "mind of the school." Aristotle stayed at the Academy for 20 years, leaving only when his beloved master died in 347 BC. In later years he renounced some of Plato's theories and went far beyond him in breadth of knowledge.

A statue of the philosopher Aristotle in his Grecian birthplace. His Meteorologica *set the standard in meteorology for 2,000 years.* Panos Karapanagiotis/Shutterstock.com

After leaving the Academy, Aristotle taught school on the coast of Asia Minor, and spent two years studying marine biology on the Greek island of Lesbos. In 342 BC, he returned to Macedonia, at the invitation of Philip II, to teach the king's young son, Alexander—who would later become Alexander the Great. No one knows how much influence the philosopher had on the headstrong youth, but after he became king, Alexander gave Aristotle enough money to set up a school in Athens.

The school in the Lyceum was a success. Aristotle called his school the Peripatetic ("to walk about") because morning discussions with his more advanced students were conducted as the group walked in the Lyceum gardens. While teaching there, Aristotle was able to collect the first great library and establish a museum.

He led his pupils in research in every existing field of knowledge. Meteorology was studied as part of his investigation of physics. As Aristotle understood it, physics was the equivalent to what would now be called "natural philosophy," or the study of nature. The science of observation was new to the Greeks, however. Hampered by lack of instruments, they were not always correct in their conclusions.

Aristotle was a victim of political maneuvering in 323 BC, when Anti-Macedonian feeling broke out in Athens. Accused of impiety, meaning he lacked the proper respect for Athenians' attitudes and teachings, Aristotle decided to leave. He was concerned that the Athenians might punish him by killing him, as they had the philosopher Socrates. He fled to Chalcis on the island of Euboea, where he died the following year.

CHAPTER 2

GALILEO

The accurate measurement of temperature developed relatively recently in human history. The invention of the thermometer is generally credited to Galileo, an Italian mathematician, astronomer, and physicist who has been called the founder of modern science.

Best known by simply his first name, Galileo Galilei was born in Pisa, Italy, on Feb. 15, 1564. Galileo was of noble birth, but his family was not rich. His father wanted him to study medicine, but Galileo preferred the physical sciences and, later, mathematics. His interests led him to discover what is known as the law of the pendulum, in 1583. He timed a swinging cathedral chandelier with his pulse and found that, regardless of whether its arc was narrow or wide, there was no difference in the time it took to complete an oscillation. This discovery led to the first reliable means of keeping time.

Astronomer and mathematician Galileo Galilei. Among Galileo's many scientific discoveries is the thermometer. Photos.com/Thinkstock

Galileo had to leave school in 1585 due to financial problems. Soon after he began work as a lecturer at the Academy of Florence, he attracted attention with discoveries in hydrostatics. His work in dynamics won him an appointment as a mathematics lecturer at the University of Pisa in 1589.

Around the time he was offered a professorship at the University of Padua (1592), Galileo devised a simple thermometer. In his instrument, the changing temperature of an inverted glass vessel produced an expansion or contraction of the air within it, which in turn changed the level of the liquid with which the vessel's long, open-mouthed neck was partially filled. This general principle was perfected in succeeding years by others who experimented with liquids such as mercury and who provided a scale to measure the expansion and contraction brought about in such liquids by rising and falling temperatures.

Galileo was not done building scientific tools. He constructed his own telescope, based on the invention of Hans Lippershey, with which he discovered, in January 1610, four satellites orbiting Jupiter. He also was able to view the surface of the moon, and examined the vast collection of stars known as the Milky Way.

While working as a mathematician and philosopher in Florence, Galileo ran afoul of the Catholic Church when he supported the work of Johannes Kepler. In 1609 Kepler published his laws of planetary motion based upon the Copernican theory that Earth rotates on its axis and that Earth and the other planets revolve around the Sun. This theory went against the church teachings. Despite receiving a formal warning from the church in 1616, Galileo continued to support Kepler and the Copernican view, most famously in a dialogue titled *The Great Systems of the Universe*.

Galileo lived out the last eight years of his life under house arrest near Florence, punished for his belief in, and teaching of, Copernican doctrine. Blinded in 1637, he continued to work until his death on Jan. 8, 1642.

CHAPTER 3

WILLIAM DAMPIER

A buccaneer, or pirate, in his early years, William Dampier later explored the western coast of Australia for the British Admiralty. He also visited the islands of New Guinea and New Britain (now part of Papua New Guinea). A keen observer of natural phenomena, Dampier was, in some respects, a pioneer in scientific exploration. One of his ship's logs contains the earliest known European description of a typhoon.

Dampier was born in East Coker, England, in August 1651. Orphaned at the age of 16, he traveled to Newfoundland (now in Canada) and later to the East Indies and the Gulf of Mexico. Between 1678 and 1691 he engaged in piracy, chiefly along the west coast of South America and in the Pacific. In 1688 he reached Australia, probably the north coast near Melville Island.

Dampier published *A New Voyage Round the World*, an account of his travels, in 1697. The book became famous and further

Explorer William Dampier was the author of the first European descriptions of a typhoon, which he witnessed in 1688 while at sea. Hulton Archive/Getty Images

popularized the idea of there being a great southern continent. Describing typhoons as "sort of violent whirlwinds," he gave the following account of a typhoon that his ship encountered in 1688:

Before these whirlwinds come on there appears a heavy cloud to the northeast which is very black near the horizon, but toward the upper part is a dull reddish color. The tempest came with great violence, but after a while, the winds ceased all at once and a calm succeeded. This lasted ... an hour, more or less, then the gales were turned around, blowing with great fury from the southwest.

In 1698 the British Admiralty appointed Dampier captain of the *Roebuck* to explore the South Seas. He sailed from England in January 1699, rounded the Cape of Good Hope, and reached an inlet off western Australia on July 26. He named this inlet Shark Bay. After exploring the coast northward to a group of islands that were from then on called the Dampier Archipelago, he went on to New Guinea and then sighted and named New Britain. With a deteriorating ship and a discontented crew, Dampier was unable to visit Australia's eastern coast, as he had intended. Instead, he continued to Java (now in Indonesia) for repairs and provisions. He sailed for England on Oct. 17, 1700, but the *Roebuck* sank off Ascension Island, in the South Atlantic, on Feb. 22, 1701. The crew remained on the island until April 3, when they were picked up by a convoy of British ships.

Back in England, Dampier was court-martialed, in part for his harsh treatment of his lieutenant, and found unfit to command any British naval ship. He made two more voyages, however, as a privateer, which is a sailor on an armed ship who attacks enemy ships for profit. He also published popular accounts of his later adventures. Dampier died in London in March 1715.

CHAPTER 4

DANIEL GABRIEL FAHRENHEIT

The German physicist Daniel Gabriel Fahrenheit invented the alcohol thermometer in 1709 and then the mercury thermometer in 1714. In 1724 he introduced the temperature scale that bears his name.

Fahrenheit was born in Gdansk, Poland, on May 24, 1686. After studying and traveling he eventually settled in Amsterdam, the Netherlands, where he became a maker of scientific instruments. He discovered a method for cleaning mercury so that it would not stick to a glass tube. This was essential to devising his mercury thermometer.

For fixed points on his temperature scale, Fahrenheit took the temperature of a mixture of ice water and salt as the low point and the human body temperature as the high point. The space between he divided into 96 degrees. He later adjusted the scale slightly so as not to have fractions for the freezing and boiling points of water. The freezing point of water then became 32° F (0° C) and the boiling point 212° F (100° C).

Fahrenheit died in the Netherlands, on Sept. 16, 1736. He is buried in The Hague, which is the seat of the Dutch government.

An early mercury thermometer, the type of thermometer invented by physicist Daniel Gabriel Fahrenheit. The instrument also uses the temperature scale introduced by, and named after, Fahrenheit. Science & Society Picture Library/Getty Images

CHAPTER 5

ANDERS CELSIUS

Swedish astronomer Anders Celsius invented the Celsius temperature scale. The scale is often called the centigrade scale because of the 100-degree interval between its defined points.

Celsius was born on Nov. 27, 1701, in Uppsala, Sweden. He was professor of astronomy at Uppsala University from 1730 to 1744. During his tenure there, in 1740, he built the Uppsala Observatory.

In 1733 Celsius published a collection of 316 observations of the aurora borealis, or northern lights, made by himself and others from 1716 to 1732. He advocated the measurement of an arc of a meridian in Lapland. In 1736 took part in an expedition organized for that purpose, which verified Isaac Newton's theory that Earth is somewhat flattened at the poles.

In 1742 Celsius described his thermometer in a paper read before the Swedish

Portrait of Anders Celsius, originator of the eponymous Celsius temperature scale. Science and Society/SuperStock

Academy of Sciences. The following formula can be used to convert a temperature from its representation on the Fahrenheit (°F) scale to the Celsius (°C) value: °C =

59(°F -32). Today, the Celsius scale is in general use wherever the metric system of units has been adopted, and it is used in scientific work everywhere.

Celsius's other works include *Dissertatio de Nova Methodo Distantiam Solis a Terra Determinandi* (1730; "A Dissertation on a New Method of Determining the Distance of the Sun from the Earth") and *De Observationibus pro Figura Telluris Determinanda in Gallia Habitis, Disquisitio* (1738; "Disquisition on Observations Made in France for Determining the Shape of the Earth"). He died on April 25, 1744, in Uppsala.

CHAPTER 6

BENJAMIN FRANKLIN

Few men have done as much for the world as Benjamin Franklin. Although he was always proud to call himself a printer, Franklin had many other talents as well. He was a diplomat, a scientist, an inventor, a philosopher, an educator, and a public servant.

Born on Jan. 17, 1706, in Boston, Mass., Franklin was apprenticed at age 12 to his brother, a local printer. He taught himself to write effectively, and in 1723 he moved to Philadelphia, where he founded the *Pennsylvania Gazette* (1729–48) and wrote *Poor Richard's Almanac* (1732–57), often remembered for its proverbs and aphorisms emphasizing prudence, industry, and honesty. He became prosperous and promoted public services in Philadelphia, including a library, a fire department, a hospital, an insurance company, and an academy that became the University of Pennsylvania. His numerous inventions include the Franklin stove and bifocal spectacles.

In his lifetime Franklin was recognized as one of the great scientific thinkers of the world. His experiments helped pioneer the understanding of electricity. When a European scientist found a way to store electricity in a special tube, Franklin ordered some of the tubes and set up a laboratory in his house. He conducted many experiments and published a book about electricity. This was one of the most widely reprinted scientific books of the time. The principles he set forth in the book formed the basis for modern electrical theory.

In 1752 he sent an account of his experiments to the Royal Society of scientists in London and to French scientists. The foreign scholars were so impressed with his work that he was elected a fellow of the Royal Society in 1756 and awarded its Copley Medal. In 1773 he was elected one of the eight foreign associates of the Royal Academy of Science in Paris.

Franklin's experiments also helped explain various weather-related phenomena, most notably lightning. Franklin realized that lightning must be a discharge of electricity from the clouds. In his book he had suggested an experiment to test this.

A Currier and Ives rendition of Benjamin Franklin's electricity experiment. A man of many talents, Franklin conducted several weather-related experiments in his lifetime. Hulton Archive/Getty Images

With the help of his son William, Franklin made the experiment in 1752. The two went to a meadow during a thunderstorm, flew a kite high in the air, and brought a charge of electricity down the kite's wet string.

Franklin noticed the loose threads of the kite string standing up. He put his knuckle to a key at his end of the string and saw an electric spark. This proved his theory that lightning is electricity.

Similar experiments had been done earlier by the French scientists to whom Franklin had sent the results of his early experiments. In honor of his scientific accomplishments, Yale, Harvard, and the College of William and Mary gave Franklin honorary degrees.

Franklin was a practical man as well as a brilliant scientific theorist. He followed up his discovery by inventing the lightning rod to protect buildings from lightning bolts.

Franklin spent the last five years of his life in Philadelphia, but even then the old inventor and statesman was not idle. He made a device for getting books down from high shelves. He wrote letters to many friends and political leaders. George Washington, Thomas Jefferson, John Adams, James Madison, and many other important Americans came to call at Franklin's house. In his last years the statesman wrote newspaper articles and his famous autobiography. His final public act was to sign a memorial to the state legislature as president of the Pennsylvania society for the abolition of black slavery.

Benjamin Franklin died at the age of 84 on April 17, 1790. After an impressive public funeral given by the city, he was buried beside his wife in Philadelphia's Christ Church cemetery.

CHAPTER 7

ALEXANDER VON HUMBOLDT

A long with Napoleon, Alexander von Humboldt was one of the most famous men of Europe during the first half of the 19th century. A German scholar and explorer whose interests encompassed virtually all of the natural and physical sciences, Humboldt laid the foundations for modern physical geography, geophysics, and biogeography, and helped to popularize science. His interest in Earth's geomagnetic fields led directly to the establishment of permanent observatories in British possessions around the world, one of the first instances of international scientific cooperation. Humboldt's meteorological data contributed to comparative climatology. The Humboldt Current off the west coast of South America (now called the Peru Current) is named after him.

Friedrich Wilhelm Karl Heinrich Alexander von Humboldt was born in Berlin, Germany (then Prussia), on Sept. 14, 1769.

Meteorological data gathered by Alexander von Humboldt during his various expeditions for-
tified the science of comparative climatology. Fotosearch/Archive Photos/Getty Images

He and his brother Wilhelm were educated at home during their early years. Wilhelm eventually became one of Europe's most noted language scholars and educational reformers.

At first Alexander was a poor student, and for some years could not decide on a career. Finally botany stirred his interest, then geology and mineralogy. He studied at the University of Göttingen and at the School of Mines in Saxony. In 1792 he obtained a position with the Prussian government's Mining Department. He worked prodigiously to improve mine safety, invented a safety lamp, and started a technical school for young miners. All the while, he was becoming convinced that his goal in life was scientific exploration.

The remainder of Humboldt's life can be divided into three segments: his expedition to South America (1799–1804); his professional life in Paris, where he organized and published the data accumulated on the expedition (1804–27); and his last years, which were spent mostly in Berlin. The Spanish government permitted him to visit Central and South America. This little-known region offered great possibilities for scientific exploration. Accompanied by the French botanist Aimé Bonpland, Humboldt covered more than 6,000 miles (9,650 kilometers) on foot and horseback, or by canoe. After the trip Humboldt went to the United States and was received by President Thomas Jefferson.

Humboldt and Bonpland returned to Europe with an immense amount of information about plants, longitude and latitude, Earth's geomagnetism, and climate. After brief visits to Berlin and a trip to Italy to inspect Mount Vesuvius, he settled in Paris, readying the 30 volumes containing the results of the South American expedition.

Humboldt returned to Berlin at the insistence of the king of Prussia. He lectured on physical geography to large audiences and organized international scientific conferences. In 1829 he traveled through Russia into Siberia, as far as the Chinese frontier. The last 25 years of his life were occupied chiefly with writing his *Kosmos*, one of the most ambitious scientific works ever published. In it Humboldt presented his cosmic view of the universe as a whole. He was writing the fifth volume of this work when he died in Berlin on May 6, 1859.

CHAPTER 8

JOHN DALTON

John Dalton, an English schoolteacher, pioneered the development of modern atomic theory. He was also hailed as the father of meteorology.

Dalton was born on Sept. 5 or 6, 1766, in Eaglesfield in Cumberland, England. In about 1780 he and his older brother, Jonathan, purchased a school in Kendal, where they taught approximately 60 students, some of them boarders. As a teacher John Dalton drew upon the experiences of two important mentors: Elihu Robinson, a Quaker gentleman of some means and scientific tastes in Eaglesfield, and John Gough, a mathematical and classical scholar in Kendal. From these men Dalton acquired the rudiments of mathematics, Greek, and Latin. Robinson and Gough were also amateur meteorologists in the Lake District, and from them Dalton gained practical knowledge in the construction and use of meteorologic instruments as well as instruction

John Dalton's first book, Meteorological Observations and Essays, *was a blend of science and common observation. The work helped legitimize meteorology as a field of scientific study.* Time & Life Pictures/Getty Images

in keeping daily weather records. Dalton retained an avid interest in meteorologic measurement for the rest of his life.

In 1793 Dalton moved to Manchester to teach mathematics. He took with him the proof sheets of his first book, a collection of essays on meteorologic topics based on his own observations together with those of his friends John Gough and Peter Crosthwaite. This work, *Meteorological Observations and Essays*, was published in 1793. It created little stir at first but contained original ideas that, together with Dalton's more developed articles, marked the transition of meteorology from a topic of general folklore to a serious scientific pursuit.

Dalton upheld the view, against contemporary opinion, that the atmosphere was a physical mixture of approximately 80 percent nitrogen and 20 percent oxygen, rather than being a specific compound of elements. He measured the capacity of the air to absorb water vapor and the variation of its partial pressure with temperature. He defined partial pressure in terms of a physical law whereby every constituent in a mixture of gases exerted the same pressure it would have if it had been the only gas present. Soon after his arrival at Manchester, Dalton was elected a member of the Manchester Literary and Philosophical Society. His first contribution to this society was a description of the defect he had discovered in his own and his brother's vision. This paper was the first publication on color blindness, which for some time thereafter was known as Daltonism.

By 1805 Dalton had advanced the atomic theory. This theory states that matter is made up of small particles called atoms, that each chemical element has its own kind of atoms (in contrast to earlier ideas that atoms are essentially alike), and that chemical changes take place between atoms or groups of atoms. To support his theory Dalton set about calculating the relative weights of the atoms of several elements. The Swedish chemist Jöns Jacob Berzelius later greatly expanded this work in a long series of experiments in which he found accurate atomic weights for about 40 elements.

After the age of 50, Dalton performed little scientific work of distinction, although he continued to pursue research in various fields. His atomic theory eventually began to prove its worth, and he gained widespread recognition. He was elected into the fellowship of the Royal Society of London and the Royal Society of Edinburgh, awarded an honorary degree from the University of Oxford, and elected as one of only eight foreign associates of the French Academy of Sciences. In Manchester he was elected president of the Literary and Philosophical Society in 1817, continuing in that office for the rest of his life. He died of a stroke in Manchester on July 27, 1844.

CHAPTER 9

JOSEPH HENRY

O ne of the first great American scientists after Benjamin Franklin, Joseph Henry aided Samuel F.B. Morse in the development of the telegraph and discovered several important principles of electricity. Henry also helped pave the way for the establishment of the U.S. Weather Bureau (later the National Weather Service).

Henry was born on Dec. 17, 1797, in Albany, N.Y. While working with electromagnets at the Albany Academy (New York) in 1829, he made important design improvements. By insulating the wire instead of the iron core, he was able to wrap a large number of turns of wire around the core and thus greatly increase the power of the magnet. He made an electromagnet for Yale College that could support 2,086 pounds (946 kilograms), a world record at the time. Although Michael Faraday is given credit for discovering electromagnetic induction — the process of converting

Portrait of Joseph Henry, the American scientist largely responsible for the creation of the U.S. Weather Bureau, known today as the National Weather Service. Hulton Archive/ Getty Images

magnetism into electricity—because he was the first to publish his results (in 1831), Henry had observed the phenomenon a year earlier.

In 1831 Henry built and successfully operated, over a distance of one mile (1.6

kilometers), a telegraph of his own design. He became professor of natural philosophy at the College of New Jersey (later Princeton University) in 1832. Continuing his research, he discovered the laws upon which the transformer is based. He also found that currents could be induced at a distance and, in one case, magnetized a needle by utilizing a lightning flash 8 miles (12 kilometers) away. This experiment was apparently the first use of radio waves across a distance. By using a thermogalvanometer, a heat-detection device, he showed that sunspots radiate less heat than the general solar surface.

In 1846 Henry became the first secretary of the Smithsonian Institution, Washington, D.C., where he organized and supported a corps of volunteer weather observers. The success of the Smithsonian meteorological work led to the creation of the U.S. Weather Bureau. One of Lincoln's chief technical advisers during the Civil War, Henry was a primary organizer of the National Academy of Sciences and its second president. He died in Washington, D.C., on May 13, 1878. In 1893 his name was given to the standard electrical unit of inductive resistance, the henry.

CHAPTER 10

CHRISTIAN DOPPLER

Austrian physicist Christian Doppler first described how the observed frequency of light and sound waves is affected by the relative motion of the source and the detector. This phenomenon became known as the Doppler effect, which is used in astronomical and meteorological measurements.

Doppler was born on Nov. 29, 1803, in Salzburg, Austria. Educated at the Polytechnical Institute in Vienna, he became director of the Physical Institute and professor of experimental physics of the University of Vienna in 1850. His earliest writings were on mathematics, but in 1842 he published *Über das farbige Licht der Doppelsterne* ("Concerning the Colored Light of Double Stars"), which contained his first statement of the Doppler effect. He theorized that since the pitch of sound from a moving source varies for a stationary observer, the color of the light from a star should alter, according to the star's velocity

Christian Doppler, after whom the meteorological phenomenon known as the Doppler effect is named. Doppler radar, which utilizes the Doppler effect, is a highly accurate weather-forecasting tool. Imagno/Hulton Archive/Getty Images

relative to Earth. Doppler died on March 17, 1853, in Venice.

Developed in the 20th century, Doppler radar can continuously measure wind speeds by observing microwaves reflected off of particles in the atmosphere, such as raindrops or dust. Doppler profiles record the apparent shift in frequency with respect to the observation point of waves emitted by a moving source. A related instrument, the radiometric profiler, observes microwaves emitted by oxygen and water vapor in the air. Careful analysis of the data yields profiles of temperature and humidity at different altitudes.

CHAPTER 11

ALEXANDER BUCHAN

B ritish meteorologist Alexander Buchan first noticed what became known as Buchan spells—departures from the normally expected temperature occurring during certain seasons. They are now believed by meteorologists to be more or less random. Buchan is credited with establishing the weather map as the basis of weather forecasting as a result of his tracing, in 1868, the path of a storm across North America and the Atlantic into northern Europe.

Buchan was born on April 11, 1829, in Kinneswood, Scotland. He took up teaching as a profession and botany as a hobby. In December 1860 he was appointed secretary of the Scottish Meteorological Society and edited and largely wrote the society's journal, thereby gaining an international reputation. In 1887 he was made a member of the Meteorological Council and in 1898 was elected a fellow of the Royal Society. In 1902 he received the first award

Although science has largely discredited his theory of "Buchan spells"—predictable, seasonal shifts in temperature—Alexander Buchan made other noteworthy contributions to the science of meteorology, chiefly the weather map. Hulton Archive/Getty Images

of the Symons Medal as the most eminent British meteorologist. He was instrumental in the opening, in 1883, of the Ben Nevis Observatory and in the discussion of the observations until it closed in 1904.

In 1867 Buchan published his *Handy Book of Meteorology*, for many years a standard textbook. In 1869 he contributed to the Royal Society of Edinburgh a paper on "The Mean Pressure of the Atmosphere and the Prevailing Winds Over the Globe, for the Months and for the Year" which secured for him a preeminent place among meteorologists. He died on May 13, 1907, in Edinburgh.

CHAPTER 12

CLEVELAND ABBE

American meteorologist Cleveland Abbe pioneered in the foundation and growth of the U.S. Weather Bureau.

Abbe was born on Dec. 3, 1838, in New York, N.Y. Trained as an astronomer, he was appointed director of the Cincinnati (Ohio) Observatory in 1868. His interest gradually turned to meteorology, however. In 1869 he began to provide regular weather forecasts using data received by telegraph.

Abbe's public weather service served as a model for the national weather service, which was organized shortly thereafter as a branch of the Signal Service. In 1871 Abbe was appointed chief meteorologist of the branch (which in 1891 was reorganized under civilian control as the U.S. Weather Bureau) and worked in that capacity for more than 45 years. Abbe died on Oct. 28, 1916, in Chevy Chase, Md. The U.S. Weather Bureau was later renamed the National Weather Service.

Cleveland Abbe, the first chief of the U.S. Weather Bureau. The bureau's weather forecasts were patterned after reports Abbe issued independently as director of the Cincinnati Observatory. Library of Congress Prints and Photographs

CHAPTER 13

WLADIMIR KÖPPEN

Russian-born German meteorologist and climatologist Wladimir Köppen is best known for his delineation and mapping of the climatic regions of the world. He played a major role in the advancement of climatology and meteorology for more than 70 years. His achievements, practical and theoretical, profoundly influenced the development of atmospheric science.

Köppen was born on Sept. 25, 1846, in St. Petersburg, Russia. His grandfather was one of the German physicians invited to Russia by the empress Catherine the Great to improve sanitation in the provinces. His father, Peter von Köppen, worked at the Academy in St. Petersburg as geographer, statistician, and historian. In gratitude for his services to Russian culture, Tsar Alexander II appointed him Academician, highest academic rank in Russia. He also granted him in 1858 a seaside estate called Karabakh on the south coast of Crimea.

His father's scholastic success and versatility inspired Köppen at an early age to apply his own intellect and perception to the varied environment of the Crimea. The complex geography of the low mountain ranges along the Black Sea coast provided the setting for his first explorations. While attending secondary school at Simferopol (1858–64), some 30 miles (48 kilometers) north of Karabakh, where the coastal ranges yield to extensive plains, he frequently traveled the mountain route inland from the sea. The floral richness and climatic variety of the region, he later emphasized, first awakened his lasting interest in the geography of the plant world and its relationship to the atmosphere.

In 1864 Köppen began his studies at the University of St. Petersburg, specializing in botany. Köppen returned to Karabakh many times, and the environmental changes he saw between the dark northern forests and the subtropical shores of the Crimea broadened his geographical perspectives.

In 1867 Köppen transferred to the University of Heidelberg, completed his doctoral dissertation on the relation of plant growth to temperature, and received his degree in 1870. A mark of Köppen's extraordinary integrity was his insistence on traveling for his final examinations from Heidelberg, where the faculty might have been prejudiced in his favor, to the University of Leipzig to assure the impartiality of his examiners.

Following the Franco-Prussian War (1870–71), in which he served in the ambulance corps, Köppen returned to St. Petersburg as assistant at the Central Physical Observatory. Three years later he accepted a position with the German Naval Observatory at Hamburg as head of the newly established division of weather telegraphy, storm warning systems, and marine meteorology. In 1879 he was given the new title of meteorologist of the observatory, and in 1884 he produced a world map of temperature belts, ranging from polar to tropical latitudes, each distinguished by the number of months having temperatures above or below certain mean values.

A major achievement in geographical climatology was reached in 1900 when Köppen introduced his mathematical system of climatic classification. Each of five major climate types was assigned a mathematical value according to temperature and rainfall. Since then, many of the systems introduced by other scholars have been based on Köppen's work.

Köppen retired from his position at the Hamburg observatory in 1919 and moved to Graz, Austria, in 1924. In 1927 he undertook, with Rudolph Geiger, the editorship of a five-volume *Handbuch der Klimatologie* ("Handbook of Climatology"), which was nearly completed when Köppen died on June 22, 1940, in Graz.

Throughout his distinguished career Köppen retained his intellectual flexibility. Well-informed on a broad range of subjects, he was keenly receptive to new ideas and methods, especially those offered by youthful scientists, who found him a patient and constructive listener. Although he was not widely traveled, he knew a great deal about the world, and he saw his work and his nonprofessional interests in full global perspective. The deep concern he felt for his fellow man was evident in the time and energy he devoted to problems of land-use reform, school reform, improved nutrition for the underprivileged, alcoholism, and calendar reform. In the cause of world peace he strongly advocated widespread use of Esperanto, which he spoke as fluently as he did German and Russian. Between 1868 and 1939 he produced more than 500 publications, some of which he translated into Esperanto.

CHAPTER 14

LÉON TEISSERENC DE BORT

French meteorologist Léon Teisserenc de Bort discovered the stratosphere. This discovery paved the way for further study of the upper atmosphere.

Teisserenc was born on Nov. 5, 1855, in Paris, France. In 1880 he began his career in the meteorological department of the Administrative Center of National Meteorology in Paris. He journeyed to Africa in 1883, 1885, and 1887 to study geology and terrestrial magnetism. In 1892 he became chief meteorologist to the center, only to resign four years later and set up his own private meteorological observatory at Trappes, near Versailles.

One of the pioneers in the use of unmanned, instrumented balloons, Teisserenc sent them up to study the characteristics of the atmosphere. He found that above an altitude of about 7 miles (11 kilometers), the atmospheric temperature remained relatively constant at all heights. In 1900 he concluded that the atmosphere must be divided into two layers: the troposphere, where the temperature changed significantly with altitude and time and therefore induced changing weather, and the stratosphere, where the temperature remained relatively stable with increased altitude and time and which he considered a region of unchanging weather conditions. Teisserenc died on Jan. 2, 1913, in Cannes, France.

CHAPTER 15

WILLIAM HENRY DINES

B ritish meteorologist William Henry Dines invented instruments to measure atmospheric properties. Among these are the anemometer and the meteorgraph.

Dines was born on Aug. 5, 1855, in London, England. The son of a meteorologist, Dines graduated from Corpus Christi College, Cambridge, with honors. He became interested in wind speed and invented a pressure-tube anemometer, the first device to measure both the velocity and direction of wind.

Dines pioneered in the use of kites and balloons for upper-air measurement, and designed a remarkable meteorograph for upper-air soundings weighing only about 2 ounces (60 grams). This became for years the standard British instrument for upper-atmosphere soundings and provided many data on pressure, temperature, and humidity in heights well into the stratosphere. His analysis of these data revealed striking

A modern anemometer, a device used to measure atmospheric properties that was invented by British meteorologist William Henry Dines. mangojuicy/Shutterstock.com

correlations between properties of the upper air and yielded valuable insights into the dynamics of cyclones and anticyclones.

Dines also added to knowledge of terrestrial and solar radiation. His collected scientific papers with a full bibliography were published in 1931 by the Royal Meteorological Society, of which he was president in 1901–02. In 1905 he was elected a fellow of the Royal Society. He died on Dec. 24, 1927, in Benson, Oxfordshire, England.

CHAPTER 16

SVANTE AUGUST ARRHENIUS

Awarded the Nobel Prize in Chemistry in 1903, Svante August Arrhenius is regarded as one of the founders of the field of physical chemistry. He was also a pioneer in studies of the greenhouse effect and constructed the first climate model of the influence of atmospheric carbon dioxide (CO_2).

Arrhenius was born on Feb. 19, 1859, in Vik, Sweden. He grew up in Uppsala, where he attended the famous Cathedral School and then entered Uppsala University, from which he received a bachelor's degree (1878) and a doctorate (1884).

Awarded a travel stipend by the Royal Swedish Academy of Sciences, he spent the period from 1886 to 1890 working with eminent scientists in other countries and refining his theory of electrolytic dissociation. This theory held that electrolytes, which dissolve in water to make a solution that conducts electricity, are separated, or

Chemist Svante August Arrhenius was among the first scientists to record the impact of carbon dioxide on the atmosphere, thereby predicting what is known as "the greenhouse effect." Science & Society Picture Library/Getty Images

dissociated, into electrically charged particles, or ions, even when no electric current is flowing through the solution. Arrhenius's theory, which represented a radically new way of approaching the study of electrolytes, was initially met with skepticism but gradually gained believers. Arrhenius also did important work on chemical reaction rates; the equation describing the dependence of reaction rates on temperature is now known as the Arrhenius equation.

Arrhenius published his climate model of the influence of atmospheric CO_2 in the *Philosophical Magazine* in 1896. Linking the calculations of his abstract model to natural processes, Arrhenius estimated the effect of the burning of fossil fuels (natural gas, coal) as a source of atmospheric CO_2. He predicted that a doubling of CO_2 due to fossil fuel burning alone would take 500 years and lead to temperature increases of 3 to 4 °C (about 5 to 7 °F). Arrhenius has since been recognized as the first to have provided a model for the effect of industrial activity on global warming.

Arrhenius was a member of the Nobel Committee for Physics of the Royal Swedish Academy of Sciences from 1901 to 1927. He received the Royal Society of London's Davy Medal in 1902, and in 1905 he became director of the Nobel Institute for Physical Chemistry at Stockholm. He died in Stockholm on Oct. 2, 1927.

CHAPTER 17

VILHELM BJERKNES

Norwegian meteorologist and physicist Vilhelm Bjerknes was one of the founders of the modern science of weather forecasting.

Bjerknes was born on March 14, 1862, in Christiania, Norway. As a youth he assisted his father, a professor of mathematics at Christiania, with research in hydrodynamics. In 1890 he went to Germany and became an assistant to and scientific collaborator with the German physicist Heinrich Hertz. Bjerknes made a comprehensive study of electrical resonance that was important in the development of radio.

After two years as lecturer at the Högskola (School of Engineering), Stockholm, Bjerknes in 1895 became professor of applied mechanics and mathematical physics at the University of Stockholm. Two years later he discovered the circulation theorems that led him to a synthesis of

His pioneering work on the theory of air masses made Norwegian meteorologist Vilhelm Bjerknes a founding father of weather forecasting. SPL/Photo Researchers, Inc.

hydrodynamics and thermodynamics applicable to large-scale motions in the atmosphere and the ocean. This work ultimately resulted in the theory of air masses, which is essential to modern weather forecasting. In 1904 he presented a farsighted program for physical weather prediction. The Carnegie Foundation awarded him an annual stipend (1905–41) to support his research.

In 1907 Bjerknes returned to Norway and accepted a professorship at the university in Kristiania (so spelled from 1877 to 1925). Five years later he became professor of geophysics at the University of Leipzig, where he organized and directed the Leipzig Geophysical Institute. In 1917 he accepted a position with a museum in Bergen, Norway, and there founded the Bergen Geophysical Institute. His most productive years were spent at Bergen; there he wrote *On the Dynamics of the Circular Vortex with Applications to the Atmosphere and to Atmospheric Vortex and Wave Motion* (1921). Now a classic, this work clearly details the most important aspects of his research.

In 1926 he obtained a position with the university in Oslo, where he continued his studies until his retirement in 1932. He died on April 9, 1951, in Oslo.

CHAPTER 18

MILUTIN MILANKOVITCH

Serbian mathematician and geophysicist Milutin Milankovitch is best known for his work that linked long-term changes in climate to astronomical factors affecting the amount of solar energy received at Earth's surface. His ideas were published in a series of papers and eventually brought together in his influential book, *Kanon der Erdbestrahlung und seine Anwendung auf das Eiszeitenproblem* (1941; "Canon of Insolation and the Ice-Age Problem").

Milankovitch was born into a large, well-to-do Serbian family on May 28, 1879, in Dalj, Austria-Hungary (now in Croatia). After local schooling, he traveled to Vienna at age 17 to study engineering at the Technische Hochshule (College of Technology). After graduation and a short hiatus for military service, he returned to Vienna and earned a doctorate in 1904 for theoretical research on concrete and the design of concrete structures. This led to a successful but short career as an engineer working on complex projects throughout the Austro-Hungarian Empire. During this period he devised and patented new approaches to concrete construction.

Portrait of Milutin Milankovitch, the mathematician and geophysicist known principally for his study of climate change triggered by solar radiation. SPL/Photo Researchers, Inc.

In 1909 Milankovitch left Vienna and took up a professorship in applied mathematics at the University of Belgrade, where he remained until retirement 46 years later. He was a popular teacher, but his true passion was research. He sought to apply his mathematical skills to areas that had not yet been extensively studied. Milankovitch wanted, he said, to find an "arable field" that he could "cultivate with my mathematical tools." He found it in meteorology, which was at the time predominantly an empirical science—that is, a science that relied on observation.

Milankovitch's goal was to calculate the temperature at different points on the surface of Earth at different times of year from axioms, or first principles. This was a formidable problem. However, his initial calculations, published in *Théorie Mathématique des phénomènes thermiques produits par la radiation solaire* (1920; "Mathematical Theory of Thermal Phenomena Caused by Solar Radiation"), gave results that were roughly in line with empirical data on present-day temperatures, and thus they immediately attracted the attention of meteorologists.

In 1924, in collaboration with German meteorologists Wladimir Köppen and Alfred Wegener, Milankovitch extended his longhand calculations hundreds of thousands of years into the past to assess the effect of known regular changes in three astronomical parameters: the obliquity (tilt) of Earth's axis of rotation, the precession (wobblelike movement) of the rotation axis, and the eccentricity (a measure of the elliptical shape) of Earth's orbit around the Sun. These three parameters govern the amount of solar radiation (insolation) that strikes Earth's surface at different latitudes in different seasons. Because they operate on different timescales, the parameters affect climate by interacting in a manner that sometimes increases and sometimes decreases the insolation at a particular location.

Milankovitch worked tirelessly to construct the radiation curves at latitudes 55°, 60°, and 65° N that appeared in *Die Klimate der geologischen Vorzeit* (1924; "Climate of the Geological Past") by Wegener and Köppen. Curves for selected lower latitudes were presented in Milankovitch's *Mathematische Klimalehre und astronomische Theorie der*

Klimaschwankungen (1930; "Mathematical Climatology and the Astronomical Theory of Climatic Changes"). Both sets of calculations were contained within his masterwork, the *Kanon of 1941*.

Milankovitch's work was challenged during the 1950s, and it soon fell out of favor. Most scientists thought that Milankovitch's predicted temperature changes were too minor to affect the advance and retreat of glaciers. Perhaps more important, several European glacial deposits that had reached ages that coincided with Milankovitch's predicted cool periods turned out not to be glacial deposits at all, and this development cast doubt on the principal evidence used to support his theory.

His work was vindicated in the 1970s, however. High-resolution studies of deep-sea cores confirmed that glacial periods, as reflected in seawater temperatures, precisely follow Milankovitch's predictions over roughly the past 1 million years. Those studies provided evidence for cyclical climate change in the past with periods of approximately 100,000, 41,000, and 23,000 years, coinciding with the astronomical cycles in eccentricity, axial tilt, and precession, respectively. The astronomically timed variations in solar radiation are now known as Milankovitch cycles.

Milankovitch was interested in making science accessible to nonscientists. For several years in the 1920s he wrote a monthly "letter" in a Serbian magazine to a young imaginary friend, in which he described mental journeys into the past to visit famous scientists and explore their ideas, especially as they related to astronomy. The letters were later collected and published as the book *Kroz vasionu i vekove: pisma jednog astronoma* (1928; "Through Distant Worlds and Times: Letters from a Wayfarer in the Universe"). Milankovitch died on Dec. 12, 1958, in Belgrade, Yugos. (now in Serbia).

CHAPTER 19

ALFRED WEGENER

In 1912 the German meteorologist Alfred Wegener proposed that throughout most of geologic time there was only one continental mass, which he named Pangaea or "All-earth," and one ocean, called Panthalassa or "All-sea." His theory is known as the continental-drift theory. Bringing together a large mass of geologic and paleontological data, Wegener suggested that Pangaea broke apart during the Jurassic Period, and the parts began to move away from one another.

Alfred Lothar Wegener was born in Berlin, Germany, on Nov. 1, 1880. The son of a director of an orphanage, he received his doctorate in astronomy from the University of Berlin in 1905. During this time he became interested in meteorology and geology. In 1906–08 he took part in an expedition to Greenland to study polar air circulation. He later made three more expeditions to Greenland, in 1912–13, 1929, and

1930, and was considered a specialist on the territory. From 1908 to 1912 he lectured at the Physical Institute in Marburg. Wegener also suggested that lunar craters arose through meteoric crashing into the Moon's surface rather than volcanic activity.

Published in 1915, his "continental-displacement" theory, as it was known, stirred an international controversy. Wegener died during his last Greenland expedition in November 1930. By that time, the continental-drift theory had been dismissed by most scientists as highly speculative. Eventually evidence was accumulated in support of the theory, partly through the study of the phenomenon known as magnetic reversal. (Studies in the 1960s indicated that Earth's magnetic field repeatedly changes polarity at intervals of 100,000 to 50 million years.) The continental-drift theory led to the concept of plate tectonics, which holds that Earth is divided into moving plates and explains the existence of volcanoes and earthquakes.

CHAPTER 20

TOR BERGERON

Swedish meteorologist Tor Bergeron is best known for his work in cloud physics.

Bergeron was born on Aug. 15, 1891, in Godstone, near London, England. He was educated at the universities of Stockholm and Oslo, from the latter of which he received his Ph.D. in 1928. He taught at the University of Stockholm (1935–45) and the University of Uppsala, Sweden (1946–60). From 1918 to 1921 he was a student and co-worker of the pioneering meteorologist Vilhelm Bjerknes and was actively engaged in the development of new methods of weather forecasting.

Bergeron was noted for his studies in the analysis of air masses and the formation of warm and cold fronts. He was also the first meteorologist to take into account upper atmospheric phenomena and their effect on weather. His theory on the

Rain from thunderclouds pouring down on the city of Singapore. Cloud physicists, such as Swedish meteorologist Tor Bergeron, study the origins and properties of precipitation droplets within clouds. coolbiere photograph/Flickr/Getty Images

origin of precipitation was instrumental in the further exploration of cloud physics. He wrote a number of works on such subjects as weather fronts, ice nuclei in clouds, methods and problems of weather forecasting, and the buildup of ice sheets. He died on June 13, 1977, in Stockholm.

CHAPTER 21

JACOB BJERKNES

The discovery by Norwegian American meteorologist Jacob Bjerknes that cyclones originate as waves associated with sloping weather fronts that separate different air masses proved to be a major contribution to modern weather forecasting.

Bjerknes was born on Nov. 2, 1897, in Stockholm, Sweden. The work of his father, the Norwegian physicist and meteorologist Vilhelm Bjerknes, influenced Bjerknes in his choice of meteorology as a career. During World War I he assisted his father in establishing a network of weather observation stations throughout Norway. Data gathered by these stations gave rise to their theory of polar fronts, essential to understanding the dynamics of weather in the middle and high latitudes. During the 1920s and 1930s, in addition to his studies of cyclones, he gathered data on the structure of low-pressure centers and conducted

Jacob Bjerknes (foreground) *visiting a hydrodynamics laboratory in Chicago.* AIP Emilio Segre Visual Archives, courtesy Dave Fultz's personal collection

research on the dynamics of atmospheric convection (heat and energy transformations in the atmosphere).

In 1939 Bjerknes moved to the United States and the next year became professor of meteorology at the University of California,

Los Angeles. After World War II his studies chiefly concerned atmospheric circulation. In 1952 he utilized photographs taken by high-altitude research rockets for weather analysis and forecasting and was thus among those who initiated the use of space-age techniques for meteorological research. In later work he discovered relationships between Pacific Ocean temperatures and North American weather. Bjerknes died on July 7, 1975, in Los Angeles.

CHAPTER 22

CARL-GUSTAF ARVID ROSSBY

Swedish American meteorologist Carl-Gustaf Arvid Rossby pioneered the study of large-scale air movement. His introduction of the equations describing atmospheric motion were largely responsible for the rapid development of meteorology as a science.

Rossby was born on Dec. 28, 1898, in Stockholm, Sweden. He moved to the United States in 1926, where he worked in Washington, D.C., as a fellow of the American-Scandinavian Foundation for Research at the U.S. Weather Bureau. In 1928 he became professor and head of the department of meteorology—the first in the United States—at the Massachusetts Institute of Technology, in Cambridge. There he made important contributions to the understanding of heat exchange in air masses and atmospheric turbulence and investigated oceanography to study the relationships between ocean currents and their effects on the atmosphere.

(a) uninterrupted upper airflow pattern

(b) waves form in polar vortex

(c) upper air waves become more pronounced

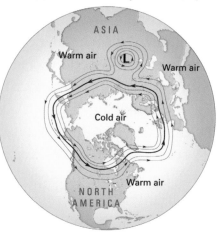

(d) initial pattern restored with the detachment of a cold air mass

H high-pressure centre
L low-pressure centre
→ jet stream

© 2007 Encyclopædia Britannica, Inc.

Graphics showing large-scale air movement over the North Pole. These air currents are called Rossby waves, named after their discoverer, Carl-Gustaf Arvid Rossby.

Rossby became a U.S. citizen in 1938. One year later he became assistant chief of the Weather Bureau in charge of research and education and began his studies of the general circulation of the atmosphere. He became chairman of the department of meteorology at the University of Chicago in 1941. In his studies he identified sinusoidal waves, now known as Rossby waves, in the polar jet stream. He also developed the theory of Rossby wave movement. He worked on mathematical models for weather prediction and introduced the Rossby equations, which were used in 1950 with an advanced electronic computer to forecast the weather.

In 1950 Rossby returned to Sweden to work with the Institute of Meteorology, which he founded in connection with the University of Stockholm. From 1954 to 1957 he was instrumental in arousing interest in atmospheric chemistry and the interaction of airborne chemicals with the land and the sea. He died on Aug. 19, 1957, in Stockholm.

CHAPTER 23

VINCENT JOSEPH SCHAEFER

In 1946 American research chemist and meteorologist Vincent J. Schaefer carried out the first systematic series of experiments to investigate the physics of precipitation. From an aircraft over Massachusetts he seeded clouds with pellets of dry ice (solid carbon dioxide) and succeeded in producing snow, initiating the science of experimental meteorology and weather control.

Vincent Joseph Schaefer was born on July 4, 1906, in Schenectady, N.Y. He attended classes at Union College in New York and graduated in 1928 from the Davey Institute of Tree Surgery. From 1933 to 1954 he worked in research at General Electric Laboratories, where his efforts during the war were directed specifically toward aircraft icing. Studies showed that when sufficient numbers of ice particles were present in clouds to eliminate the hazardous supercooled water conditions, ice

Modern cloud-seeding in action, with pellets or "seeds" being dispensed from the machinery attached to the plane's wing. © Minden Pictures/SuperStock

ceased to form on airplane bodies. Using dry ice, Schaefer discovered by chance how to produce this condition artificially.

In 1959 Schaefer joined the faculty of the State University of New York at Albany and was professor of atmospheric science there from 1964 to 1976. He was appointed fellow of the American Academy of Arts and Sciences, and he received an award in 1957 and a special citation in 1976 from the American Meteorological Society. He died on July 25, 1993, in Schenectady.

CHAPTER 24

WALTER MUNK

Austrian-born American oceanographer Walter Munk's pioneering studies of ocean currents and wave propagation laid the foundations for contemporary ocean-ography. Munk also played a leading role in researching the implications of global warming for the oceans.

Munk was born on Oct. 19, 1917, in Vienna. He moved to Lake George, N.Y., in 1932 to attend boarding school, as his parents hoped to prepare him for a career in banking. He worked in banking for several years but grew dissatisfied and left to take classes at Columbia University. After earning a bachelor's degree (1939) in physics from the California Institute of Technology, Munk convinced Harald Sverdrup, director of the Scripps Institution of Oceanography at the University of California, Los Angeles, to give him a summer job. By 1940 he had earned a master's degree in geophysics from the California Institute of Technology and by 1947 had completed a doctorate in oceanography at Scripps. After graduation Scripps hired him as an assistant professor of geophysics. He became a full professor there in 1954 and was made a member of the University of California's Institute of Geophysics.

Distressed by the 1938 occupation of Austria by Germany, Munk had applied for U.S. citizenship and enlisted in the U.S. Army prior to completing his doctorate. From 1939 to 1945 he joined several of his colleagues from Scripps at the U.S. Navy Radio and Sound Laboratory, where they developed methods related to amphibious warfare. Their method for predicting and dealing with waves was carried out success-fully by the Allied forces on D-Day (June 6, 1944) during the Normandy invasion.

Following the war, in 1946, Munk helped to analyze the currents, diffusion, and water exchanges at Bikini Atoll in the South Pacific, where the United States was testing nuclear weapons. Funded by a Guggenheim Fellowship, he spent a portion of 1949 at the University of Oslo studying the dynamics of ocean currents. Throughout the 1950s Munk studied the effect of geophysical processes on the wobble in Earth's rotation, publishing the seminal results in *The Rotation of the Earth: A Geophysical Discussion* (with G.J.F. MacDonald, 1960).

In 1959 Munk began campaigning for the creation of what would become the Cecil H. and Ida M. Green Institute of Geophysics and Planetary Physics (IGPP) at Scripps. He directed the institute until 1982. From 1965 to 1975 Munk worked on the Mid-Ocean Dynamics Experiment (MODE), which resulted in significant improvement in the accuracy of tide prediction. *Waves Across the Pacific*, a 1967 documentary, depicted his study of how waves generated by storms in the Southern Hemisphere travel through the rest of the world's oceans. In 1968 he became a member of JASON, a panel of scientists who advised the U.S. government.

Beginning in 1975, Munk had begun experimenting with the use of acoustic tomography, which uses sound waves to generate images of water. This culminated in the 1991 Heard Island experiment, in

Oceanographer Walter Munk, receiving the 2010 Crafoord Prize in geophysics. Munk has made several important discoveries while studying the connection between ocean currents and the weather. Jonas Ekstromer/AFP/Getty Images

which sound signals were transmitted from instruments 492 feet (150 meters) below the ocean's surface to receivers around the world. The project used the speed at which the signals transmitted to measure the temperature of the water. He cowrote the definitive volume on the subject, *Ocean Acoustic Tomography* (1995).

Munk was named Secretary of the Navy Research Chair in Oceanography in 1984 and continued to examine the effects of global warming on the oceans as part of the Acoustic Thermometry of Ocean Climate (ATOC) project from 1996 to 2006. In the early 21st century Munk and colleague Peter Wadhams of the University of Cambridge estimated that the warming of the oceans was causing a rise in sea level of about 0.5 millimeters (1 millimeter = about 0.04 inches) per year and that glacial melting contributed about another 0.6 millimeters per year—resulting in a total rate of 1.1 millimeters per year. Other researchers calculated higher rates.

Munk was the recipient of the Royal Astronomical Society's 1968 Gold Medal and the American Geophysical Union's

1989 William Bowie Medal, among others. He became the first recipient of the annual Walter Munk Award, given in his honor by the Oceanography Society and several naval offices, in 1993. In 1999 he won the 15th annual Kyoto Prize in Basic Sciences for his work in physical oceanography and geophysics; he became the first in his field to be honored with this award.

CHAPTER 25

T. THEODORE FUJITA

Japanese-American meteorologist T. Theodore Fujita created the Fujita Scale, or F-Scale, a system of classifying tornado intensity based on damage to structures and vegetation. He also discovered macrobursts and microbursts, weather phenomena that are associated with severe thunderstorms and are hazards to aviation.

Tetsuya Theodore Fujita was born on Oct. 23, 1920, in Kitakyushu City, Japan. He earned a bachelor's degree in mechanical engineering in 1943 from Meiji College of Technology, Tokyo, Japan, where he became an assistant professor in the physics department in 1944. Upon completion of a doctoral degree from Tokyo University in 1953, he moved to the United States and joined the meteorology department at the University of Chicago. After a trip to Japan in 1955–56 to obtain an immigrant visa, he returned to the University of Chicago. He

T. Theodore Fujita conjures up a storm using a tornado simulator. The tornado classification scale, which determines wind intensity and damage potential, is named for Fujita. © AP Images

remained there, serving in a variety of positions, until his death on Nov. 19, 1998.

Early in his career, Fujita turned his attention to tornadoes, a subject of lifelong fascination. He made extensive use of aerial surveys of tornado tracks and took innumerable aerial photographs, displaying an uncanny ability to discern order and pattern in jumbles of debris and downed trees. His post-event analyses of tornadoes were holistic, bringing together not only traditional meteorological data on temperatures and winds but also photography of damaged structures, photogrammetric analyses of movies of tornadoes to estimate the magnitude of the swirling winds, analysis of bounce and drag marks on the surface, and observation of directions in which trees had been uprooted and debris and detritus thrown. The resulting reports with their detailed mappings told simple, clear stories about one of nature's most powerful events. Fujita's detailed maps of tornado tracks were hand-drawn, reportedly because he did not trust computers for such fine-scale work.

He introduced the concept of the tornado "family," a sequence of tornadoes, each with a unique path, produced by a single thunderstorm over a few hours. Prior to this, long damage paths were commonly attributed to a single tornado that sometimes "skipped" along its path.

Fujita's analysis of the Palm Sunday Outbreak of April 11–12, 1965—during which a six-state area of Ohio, Michigan, Indiana, Illinois, Wisconsin, and Iowa in the United States was severely damaged by a series of tornadoes—was the first systematic analysis of a regional outbreak. Based on this study and an airborne observation of a large dust devil, he put forth the concept of the "multiple vortex tornado," that is, a system of smaller vortices circling around a common center. These small embedded vortices—sometimes termed suction vortices—are often found in the most violent tornadoes and may contain the highest wind speeds known (greater than 300 miles per hour, or 500 kilometers per hour).

His study of damage in the Palm Sunday Outbreak also led directly to his intensity scale for characterizing tornadoes. The F-Scale is now used internationally to estimate tornado intensity based upon severity of damage to buildings and vegetation.

The capstone of Fujita's work with tornadoes is considered by many to have been his work with the Super Outbreak of April 3–4, 1974, a national-scale outbreak of 148 tornadoes (four of these tornadoes were later reclassified as downbursts by Fujita) that caused severe damage to the

Midwestern and Eastern United States and Ontario, Can. His maps of complex damage patterns aided his identification of a previously undiscovered phenomena, the downburst and the microburst. These sudden, severe downdrafts can result in 150-mile- (250-kilometer-) per-hour winds on or near the ground that often uproot trees in discernible starburst patterns. In the face of widespread skepticism among his colleagues, Fujita insisted that these damage patterns were the products of columns of air descending rapidly from a thunderstorm, striking the surface, and then flowing out in all directions.

Fujita received national attention in 1975 when he linked an airliner crash at New York's Kennedy Airport to microbursts. Subsequent studies showed conclusively that sudden downdrafts from thunderstorms were indeed a previously unappreciated aviation hazard, a finding that led to installation of special Doppler radars at major commercial airports to improve safety. Much of Fujita's later work was devoted to describing how these downdrafts interact with aircraft during takeoff and landing.

Fujita also studied other forms of severe weather, such as thunderstorms and hurricanes. He pioneered novel techniques for analyzing small to midsized weather conditions, laying the foundation for the "mesoscale analyses" now carried out in weather stations all over the world. He introduced the basic concepts of thunderstorm architecture, including terms such as "wall cloud" and "tail cloud" that are in widespread use today.

CHAPTER 26

BERT BOLIN

S wedish meteorologist Bert Bolin was the founding chairman (1988–97) of the UN Intergovernmental Panel on Climate Change (IPCC), an international organization of some 2,000 scientists. In 2007 the IPCC shared, with former U.S. vice president Al Gore, the Nobel Peace Prize for "efforts to build up and disseminate greater knowledge about man-made climate change, and to lay the foundations for the measures that are needed to counteract such change."

Bolin was born on May 15, 1925, in Nyköping, Sweden. He graduated (1946) from Uppsala University and studied meteorology (M.S., 1949; Ph.D., 1956) at Stockholm University. As a professor of meteorology (1961–90) at Stockholm, he did significant fundamental research into the carbon cycle in nature. His ability to articulate his research findings and the threat posed by climate change earned him

Swedish meteorologist Bert Bolin led the IPCC, which in 2007 was awarded the Nobel Peace Prize, along with former U.S. vice president Al Gore, for furthering the public's knowledge concerning climate change. © AP Images

numerous honors, as well as his position with the IPCC and the post of scientific director at the European Space Agency. Bolin's final book, *A History of the Science and Politics of Climate Change: The Role of the Intergovernmental Panel on Climate Change*, was published shortly before his death on Dec. 30, 2007, in Stockholm.

CHAPTER 27

CHARLES DAVID KEELING

American scientist Charles David Keeling presented the first evidence that carbon dioxide produced by automobiles and factories was negatively affecting Earth's climate. He devised what has become known as the Keeling Curve, a graph showing seasonal and annual changes in atmospheric carbon dioxide (CO_2) concentrations since 1958 at the Mauna Loa Observatory in Hawaii.

Keeling was born on April 20, 1928, in Scranton, Pa. In 1958 he began measuring atmospheric CO_2 with instruments that he set up on Mauna Loa, a dormant volcano. Atmospheric CO_2 concentrations were calculated daily by using infrared gas analyzers, instruments that convert infrared absorbance in each sample to CO_2 concentrations in parts per million (ppm), and their values were charted.

In aggregate, the Keeling Curve shows an annual rise in atmospheric CO_2

Charles David Keeling, posing at his laboratory at the Scripps Institute of Oceanography. Keeling is responsible for charting levels of carbon dioxide in the atmosphere, which greatly influences climate change. San Diego Union-Tribune/ZUMAPresscom

concentrations. The curve shows that average concentrations have risen from about 316 parts per million by volume (ppmv) of dry air in 1959 to approximately 370 ppmv in 2000 and 390 ppmv in 2010. Average concentrations rose by 1.3 to 1.4 ppmv per year until the mid-1970s, from which time they increased by roughly 2 ppmv per year.

The year-to-year increase in atmospheric CO_2 concentrations is roughly proportional to the amount of CO_2 released into the

The Keeling Curve

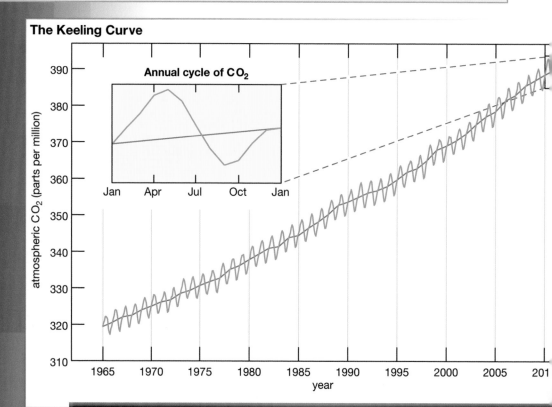

The Keeling Curve, named after American climate scientist Charles David Keeling. The graph charts the buildup of CO_2 in the atmosphere. Encyclopædia Britannica, Inc.

atmosphere by the burning of fossil fuels. Between 1959 and 1982, the rate of CO_2 emissions from fossil-fuel combustion doubled from approximately 2.5 billion tons of carbon equivalent per year to 5 billion tons of carbon equivalent per year. This increase in emissions is reflected in the curve by a slight increase in the slope over the period. The shape of the curve has also allowed scientists to conclude that approximately 57 percent of CO_2 emissions remain in the atmosphere from year to year.

The curve also captures seasonal changes in atmospheric CO_2 concentration. The curve reveals that CO_2 concentrations decrease during periods corresponding to the spring and summer months in the Northern Hemisphere. This decline is explained by the rapid leafing of vegetation during the early spring and subsequent plant growth in the summer, when the influence of photosynthesis is greatest. (Photosynthesis removes CO_2 from the air and converts it, along with water and other minerals, into oxygen and organic compounds that can be used for plant growth.) When spring arrives in the Northern Hemisphere, the portion of the planet that contains most of the land area and vegetation cover, the increased rate of photosynthesis outpaces the production of CO_2, and a decrease in carbon dioxide concentrations can be observed in the curve. As photosynthetic rates slow in the Northern Hemisphere during the autumn and winter months, atmospheric CO_2 concentrations rise.

The Keeling Curve serves as a link between modern CO_2 concentrations and those of the past. The data in the curve can be compared with the carbon dioxide concentrations of air bubbles trapped in ice cores. Such comparisons reveal that for most of the period between 1000 and 2000 CE, CO_2 concentrations fluctuated between about 275 and 290 ppmv. Since about 1900, however, levels have risen steadily, reaching the level of 390 ppmv in 2010 shown in the Keeling Curve. The results of numerous studies reveal the close association between atmospheric CO_2 concentrations and near-surface air temperature. Ice-core studies also reveal that the timing of ice ages and warm periods parallels the rise and fall of atmospheric CO_2.

The Keeling Curve is the longest uninterrupted instrumental record of atmospheric CO_2 in the world, and it is commonly regarded as one of the best and most recognizable products of a long-term scientific study. The curve is considered by many scientists to be a trustworthy measure of CO_2 in the middle layers of the troposphere, and it has been interpreted by many climate scientists as a warning signal for global warming.

In 2002 Keeling was awarded the National Medal of Science. He died on June 20, 2005, in Hamilton, Mont.

CHAPTER 28

JANE LUBCHENCO

I n 2009 American environmental scientist and marine ecologist Jane Lubchenco became the first woman to serve as administrator of the National Oceanic and Atmospheric Adminstration (NOAA) and as U.S. undersecretary of commerce for oceans and atmosphere.

Lubchenco was born on Dec. 4, 1947, in Denver, Colo. She received a bachelor's degree in biology (1969) from Colorado College. She obtained a master's degree in zoology (1971) from the University of Washington and a doctorate in ecology (1975) from Harvard University. Her thesis work focused on community structure in coastal rockpools. She served as an assistant professor at Harvard from 1975 to 1977. In 1977 she began teaching marine biology at Oregon State University and the following year became a research associate at the Smithsonian Institution, a position she held

National Oceanic and Atmospheric Administration head Jane Lubchenco, addressing journalists during a White House press conference in 2010. Jim Watson/AFP/Getty Images

until 1984. Her areas of research included algal ecology, plant-herbivore and predator-prey interactions, global change community structure, and the evolutionary ecology of individuals. She continued to teach at Oregon State, receiving an endowed chair in 1995.

Lubchenco served as president of the Ecological Society of America (1992–93). Later, she was chair of the task force on the environment (1998–2000) at the National Science Board and an adviser (1996–2000) to Religion, Science, and the Environment, a cross-disciplinary partnership of scientists and religious leaders. She was president of the International Council for Science from 2002 to 2005. Lubchenco held memberships in the National Academy of Sciences (1996), the American Philosophical Society (1998), and other prestigious organizations.

Recognizing that environmental change did not come about without mass participation, Lubchenco sought ways to better inform the public of scientific issues and to bridge the gulf between researchers and the rest of the world. In a 1997 speech she proposed the idea of a social contract between scientists and society. Lubchenco founded the Aldo Leopold Leadership Program, aimed at enhancing the ability of research scientists to communicate their findings to a general audience, in 1998, and she helped to create the Communication Partnership for Science and Sea (COMPASS), an organization devoted to educating policy makers on ocean ecology, in 1999. That year she also helmed the Partnership for Interdisciplinary Studies of Coastal Oceans (PISCO). Lubchenco was one of the primary organizers (2008–09) of Climate Central, which focused on disseminating information on climate change to the public.

Lubchenco's ability to combine passionate advocacy with pragmatism led to her nomination as NOAA administrator and undersecretary of commerce for oceans and atmosphere by Pres. Barack Obama in December 2008. She was confirmed in March 2009 to wide approval from the scientific community.

CONCLUSION

Recent technological advances have greatly aided the work of meteorologists and climatologists as they continue to research atmospheric processes around the world and the causes of climatic differences and changes. Weather satellites now monitor the global atmosphere almost continuously, adding immense amounts of information to the meteorologist's daily data base. Not only do satellites provide photographs that make it possible to detect and track weather systems from the moment they begin to form, but remote sensors mounted on satellites also send back streams of data on atmospheric conditions.

Virtually every segment of society today benefits from weather forecasts: the aviation, maritime, and energy industries; water-management and pollution-control agencies; farmers and agricultural organizations; and, of course, the general public. Moreover, accurate weather forecasts are becoming increasingly important. Thus most governments, many universities, and some private corporations sponsor meteorological research programs that range from investigations of the atmosphere to studies that search for improved methods for predicting the weather. Currently researchers are trying to develop computer models that will provide accurate forecasts of weather conditions as many as 30 days in advance.

Improved radar systems for detecting and monitoring hazardous weather conditions are under development, and other new systems will provide meteorologists and climatologists with a continuous profile of atmospheric conditions. Advanced satellites will monitor the space extending from the Sun to Earth, including Earth's magnetosphere, ionosphere, and atmosphere. Recently the field of meteorology has expanded to include the study of other planetary atmospheres as well. All of these technological advances will no doubt assist and inspire the next generation of pioneers in the fields of meteorology and climatology.

GLOSSARY

amphibious Occurring on both land and water.

anemometer An instrument for measuring and indicating the force or speed of the wind.

botany A branch of biology dealing with plant life.

climatology The study of climates and meteorological phenomena.

cyclone A weather system marked by strong rotating winds, often forming a destructive funnel of wind and rain.

deep-sea core A narrow column of sample material taken from the ocean bottom for research and experimentation.

downdraft A strong, downward current of air that occurs during serious storms.

greenhouse effect The trapping of heat (infrared radiation) from the Sun and re-emitted by Earth's surface in the lower levels of the atmosphere by carbon dioxide, water vapor, and certain other gases.

lightning rod A grounded metallic rod set up on a building or structure to protect it from lightning.

macroburst A violent, short-lived down-draft accompanied by extreme wind shears that covers a larger area than a microburst; usually associated with thunderstorms.

meteorology Scientific study of atmospheric phenomena, particularly of the troposphere and lower stratosphere.

microburst A violent, short-lived, localized downdraft that creates extreme wind shears at low altitudes, usually associated with thunderstorms.

oscillation The act of swinging or moving to and fro, as a pendulum.

photogrammetric Having to do with the science of making reliable measurements using photographs, especially aerial photographs.

prodigious Something that occurs in great quantity of great degree; awe-inspiring.

sinusoidal Of, relating to, shaped like, or varying according to a sine curve or sine wave; characterized by side-to-side movement.

stratosphere Layer of the atmosphere above the troposphere.

sunspots Cooler spots on the surface of the Sun that appear dark and are connected to magnetic field activity.

tomography An imaging technique that uses data from sound waves to form three-dimensional representations of solid objects.

troposphere The region on Earth where nearly all water vapor exists and essentially all weather occurs.

turbulence Irregular atmospheric motion, especially when characterized by up-and-down currents.

typhoon A violent tropical storm occurring over the west Pacific and Indian oceans; known as a hurricane when occurring over the North Atlantic and northeast Pacific oceans.

velocity The quantity that designates how fast and in what direction a point is moving.

vortex The cavity or hollow core found at the center of a swirling mass of fluid or air.

weather front A boundary area between air masses of differing temperatures.

American Meteorological Society
45 Beacon Street
Boston, MA 02108-3693
(617) 227-2425
Web site: http://www.ametsoc.org
Founded in 1919, the American Meteorological
     Society provides information and educa-
     tion on atmospheric and oceanic sciences
     through numerous conferences, programs,
     and services, as well as journals.

Canadian Meteorological and
     Oceanographic Society
360 Laurier Avenue
Ottawa, ON K1P 1C8
Canada
(613) 990-0300
Web site: http://www.cmos.ca
The Canadian Meteorological and
     Oceanographic Society is dedicated
     to advancing atmospheric and oceanic
     sciences and related environmental
     disciplines in Canada. Information
     and publications cover meteorological
     aspects of agriculture, forestry, and
     meteorological phenomena.

Environment Canada
351 St. Joseph Boulevard
Place Vincent Massey, 8th Floor
Gatineau, QC K1A 0H3
Canada
(819) 997-2800
Web site: http://www.climatechange.gc.ca
Environment Canada provides information on the basics of climate and climate change, as well as reports detailing the various issues Canadians face as a result of climate change and potential solutions.

National Oceanic and Atmospheric Administration
1401 Constitution Avenue NW
Room 5128
Washington, DC 20230
(301) 713-1208
Web site: http://www.noaa.gov
The National Oceanic and Atmospheric Administration provides information about opportunities to advance environmental literacy, including workshops for educators and scholarships and internships for students.

National Weather Association
228 West Millbrook Road
Raleigh, NC 27609-4304
(919) 845-1546
Web site: http://www.nwas.org
The National Weather Association is a
    nonprofit professional association of
    meteorologists. The group provides
    publications and workshops, as well
    as various outreach, educational, and
    training initiatives to students, users
    of weather information, and the
    general public.

World Meteorological Organization
7bis, avenue de la Paix,
Case postale No. 2300, CH-1211
Geneva 2, Switzerland
+ 41(0)22 7308111
Web site: http://www.wmo.int
A specialized agency of the United
    Nations based in Switzerland, the
    World Meteorological Organization
    promotes international cooperation
    between the world's meteorological
    stations. The organization seeks to
    standardize meteorological observations,

encourage research and training, and extend the use of meteorological findings to different fields.

WEB SITES

Due to the changing nature of Internet links, Rosen Publishing has developed an online list of Web sites related to the subject of this book. This site is updated regularly. Please use this link to access the list:

http://www.rosenlinks.com/inven/weathpi

BIBLIOGRAPHY

Alberti, Theresa Jarosz. *Climates* (Capstone Press, 2005).

Farndon, John. *Extreme Weather* (DK Publishing, 2007).

Gallant, Roy A. *Atmosphere: Sea of Air* (Benchmark Books, 2003).

Herman, Gail, and Schwinger, Larry. *Storm Chasers: Tracking Twisters* (Grossett & Dunlap, 1997).

Kahl, Jonathan D. *Weather Watch: Forecasting the Weather* (Lerner Publications, 1996).

Mack, Lorrie. *Weather* (DK Publishing, 2004).

Mahaney, Ian F. *Climate Maps* (PowerKids Press, 2007).

Stevermer, Amy J. *Recent Advances and Issues in Meteorology* (Oryx Press, 2002).

Walker, Sally M., and Flannery, Tim F. *We Are the Weather Makers: The History of Climate Change* (Candlewick Press, 2009).

Wills, Susan, and Wills, Steven R. *Meteorology: Predicting the Weather* (Oliver Press, 2004).

INDEX

A

Abbe, Cleveland, 52–53
Acoustic Thermometry
of Ocean Climate
(ATOC) project, 92
air masses, theory of, 67
Aldo Leopold Leadership
Program, 110
anemometers, 61
Aristotle, 12–15
Arrhenius, Svante, 63–65
Arrhenius equation, 65

B

Bergen Geophysical
Institute, 68
Bergeron, Tor, 77–79
Berzelius, Jöns Jacob, 41
Bjerknes, Jacob, 80–82
Bjerknes, Vilhelm, 66–68,
77, 80
Bolin, Bert, 100–101
Bonpland, Aimé, 37
Buchan, Alexander, 49–51
Buchan spells, 49

C

Carnegie Foundation, 67
Cecil H. and Ida M. Green
Institute of Geophysics

and Planetary Physics
(IGPP), 90
Celsius, Anders, 26–28
Celsius temperature
scale, 26–28
Climate Central, 111
cloud seeding, 86
color blindness, 41
Communication
Partnership for
Science and Sea
(COMPASS), 110–111
continental-drift theory,
75, 76
Copernican theory, 19
Crosthwaite, Peter, 40

D

Dalton, John, 38–42
Daltonism, 41
Dampier, William, 20–23
Dampier Archipelago, 22
Dines, William, 61–62
Doppler, Christian,
46–48
Doppler effect, 46
Doppler radar, 48, 98

E

electrolytic dissolution,
theory of, 63–65